special kind of work. Cells carry water. They make and store food. They start the

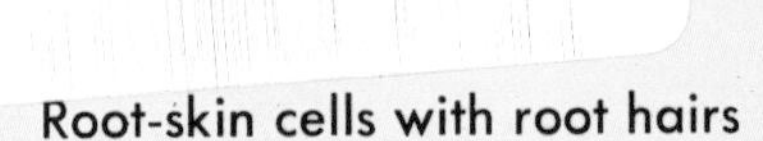

Root-cap cells on young root

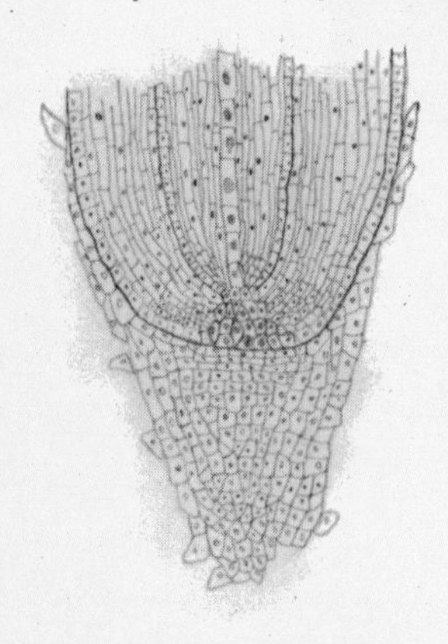

Root-skin cells with root hairs

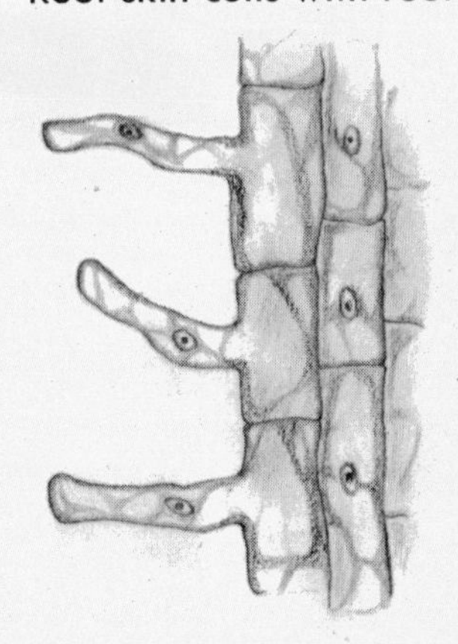

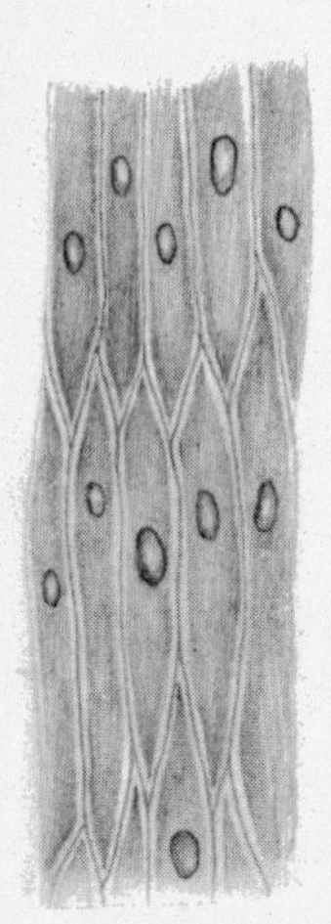

Cambium cells grow into wood and bark

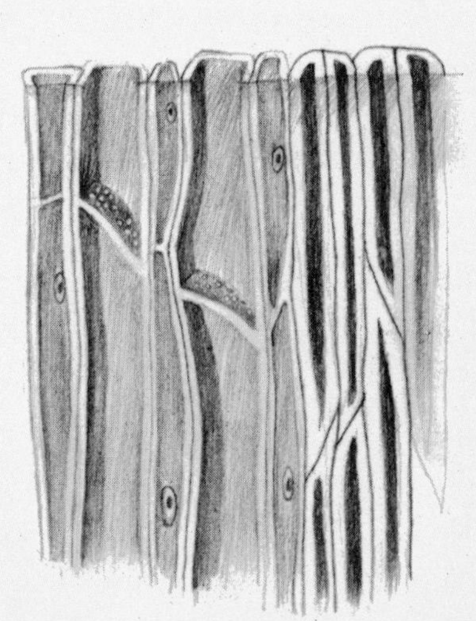

Bark cells

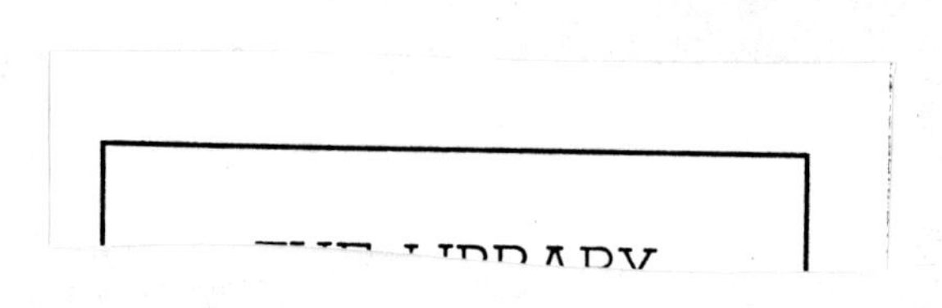

WHAT'S INSIDE OF PLANTS?

by **HERBERT S. ZIM**

illustrated by

HERSCHEL WARTIK

WILLIAM MORROW & CO. NEW YORK, 1952

Foreword

In this first book of botany for young people I have tried to explain in text and pictures the parts and workings of plants we all know. The book can be used in many ways: very young readers can discover facts from the pictures alone; older readers will find the large-type text of further help; the detailed text, in smaller type, is for adults to read to children and for young people who are better readers.

My thanks to Professor Oswald Tippo, Chairman, Department of Botany, University of Illinois, Urbana, Illinois, for checking the manuscript and illustrations.

H.S.Z.

 Published simultaneously in the Dominion of Canada by George J. McLeod, Limited, Toronto.
Library of Congress Catalog Card Number: 52-5943

WHAT'S INSIDE OF PLANTS?

There are thousands of kinds of plants. Some are so small you can hardly see them. Other plants are the largest living things. The kinds of plants we see most often are the flowering plants. Peas, beans, corn, roses, and tomatoes are flowering plants. Most trees are flowering plants, too. All flowering plants have leaves. They also have stems, roots, flowers, and fruits. Some are woody and grow for many years. Some grow one year and bloom the next. Some live and die in a single summer.

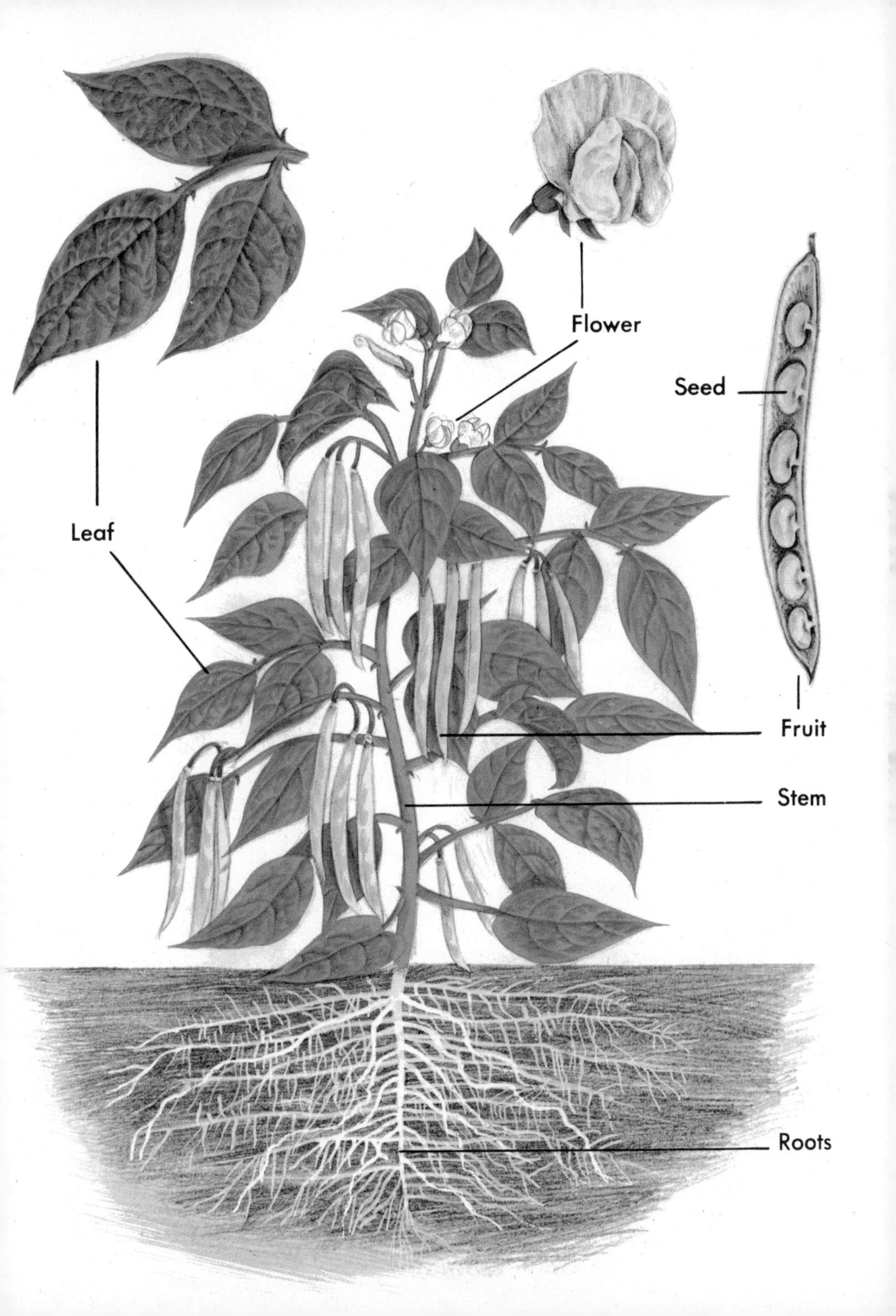
Flower
Seed
Leaf
Fruit
Stem
Roots

Nearly all the common plants of gardens, fields, and woods are flowering plants. These plants usually grow from seeds. As the seed sprouts, the small plant or seedling quickly grows roots, stems, and leaves. These three parts make up most of the plants you see. As the plants grow older, they have flowers which ripen into seeds and fruits.

The smallest flowering plant is less than a quarter of an inch long. The largest ones are trees hundreds of feet high. In all these different plants, the roots, stems, and leaves do the work of keeping the plant alive and growing. Every part of a small plant is likely to be alive and growing. When you eat a raw carrot, an apple, or lettuce, you are eating living parts of plants. These parts are alive even though they have been picked from the plant and are not growing. The center of the trunk of a large tree is dead. The parts of the trunk near the bark, the roots, and the leaves are alive.

Like all living things, plants need food, air, water, and warmth. In the sunlight, a plant can make its own food. This is something that only plants can do. Plants also need air; even plants that live in water need it. They use the air that dissolves in water just as sugar dissolves in a cup of tea. The temperature must be above freezing for plants to grow, but plants can also grow in the hottest deserts. When plants have food, air, water, warmth, and sunlight they live and grow. Their flowers ripen into fruits and from the seeds new plants begin.

WHAT'S INSIDE A LEAF?

Black locust

Black oak

Dogwood

Horse chestnut

GERANIUM LEAF

Silver maple

Banana (8-9 feet long)

Leaves make food for plants. The green coloring in them does the work when the sun is shining. Water comes to the leaves through tiny tubes from the roots and stems. Air enters the leaves through very small holes. Leaves use water and a gas from the air to make food. This food is stored in other parts of the plant. You eat it when you eat apples, potatoes, or corn. Milk and meat come from animals that eat plant food. Without green plants, animals and people could not live.

INSIDE A LEAF

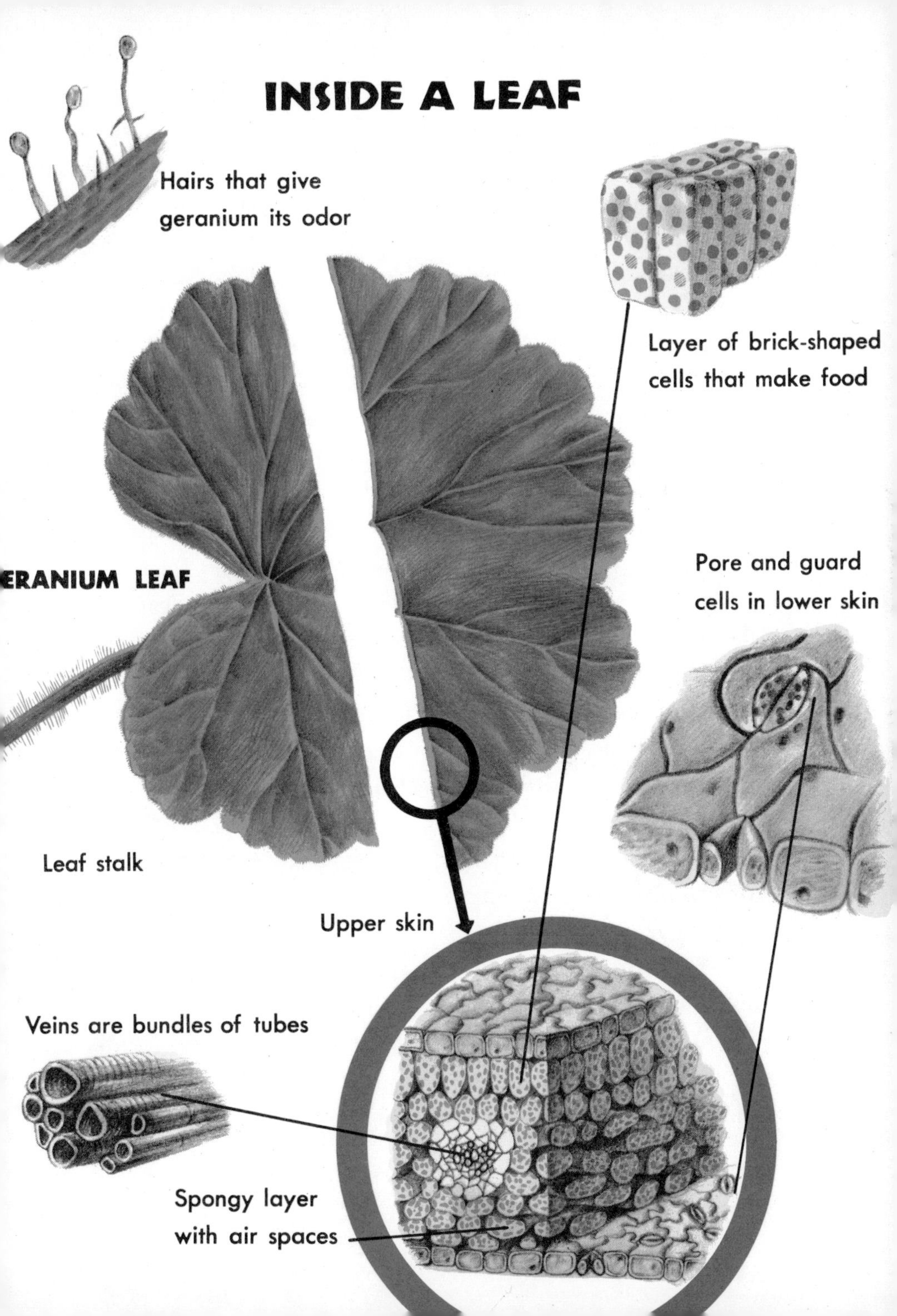

Green plants are the most important of all living things. Like all other living things, plants and their leaves are made of cells. Cells are usually very small, yet each one is alive. They are the smallest living parts of living things. In a single corn plant there are billions of cells. Thousands upon thousands of them make up a single leaf. Each leaf cell contains tiny green specks. These make food for the plant—food that animals eat too. When the sun shines, the green color in the leaves makes the water and carbon dioxide gas in the leaf join together into a kind of sugar. Later the plant changes some of this sugar into other kinds of food. Corn picked fresh from the garden tastes sweeter because it has more sugar in it. So do peas and other garden vegetables.

The food that plants make helps them to grow. The cells that make the roots, stems, flowers, and new leaves use the food the leaves make. Plants also take in minerals from the soil. They need these minerals to grow. But minerals and fertilizers are not plant food. Plants make their own food.

The leaf of a plant has an outer skin (called epidermis). This protects the leaf and keeps it from drying out. This skin, especially on the underside of the leaf, is pierced by thousands of small holes, or pores, each one guarded by a pair of cells. These cells open the pores when the plant is in sunlight. They close at night and so control the movement of water in the plant. The layer of long cells near the top of the leaf does most of the work in food making.

WHAT'S INSIDE OF STEMS?

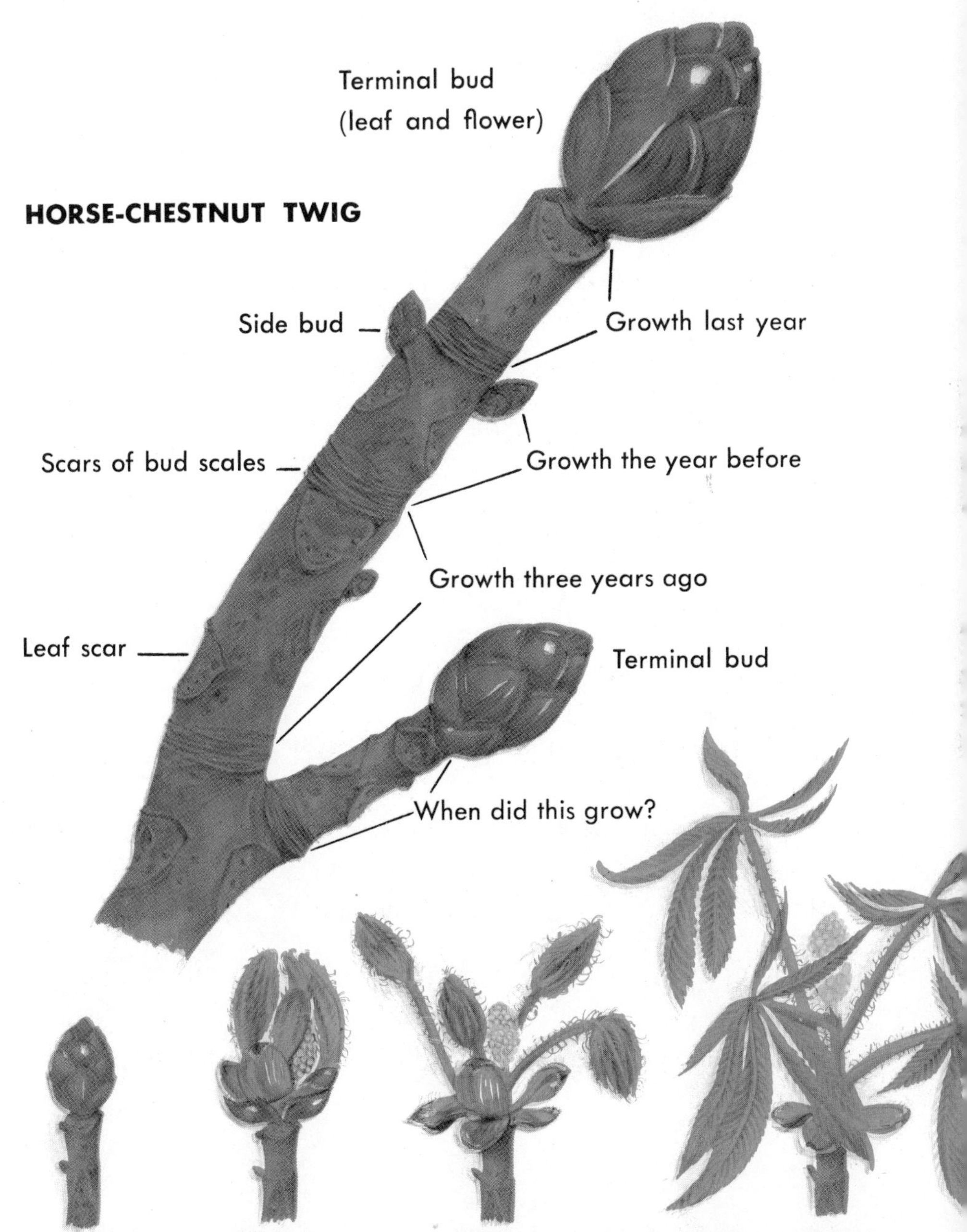

Put a horse-chestnut twig in water. Watch the buds open

Water moves up and food moves down the stem in rings of long tubes. These tubes are like very small pipes. They are formed from living cells in the growing stem. The tubes join the veins of leaves. They go from the leaves, through the twigs and trunk, all the way down to the roots. A stem grows longer only at the tip, but every part of a stem grows thicker. Most stems grow thick faster in the spring, forming a ring of larger tubes. The rings in a stump tell the age of the tree.

INSIDE OF STEMS

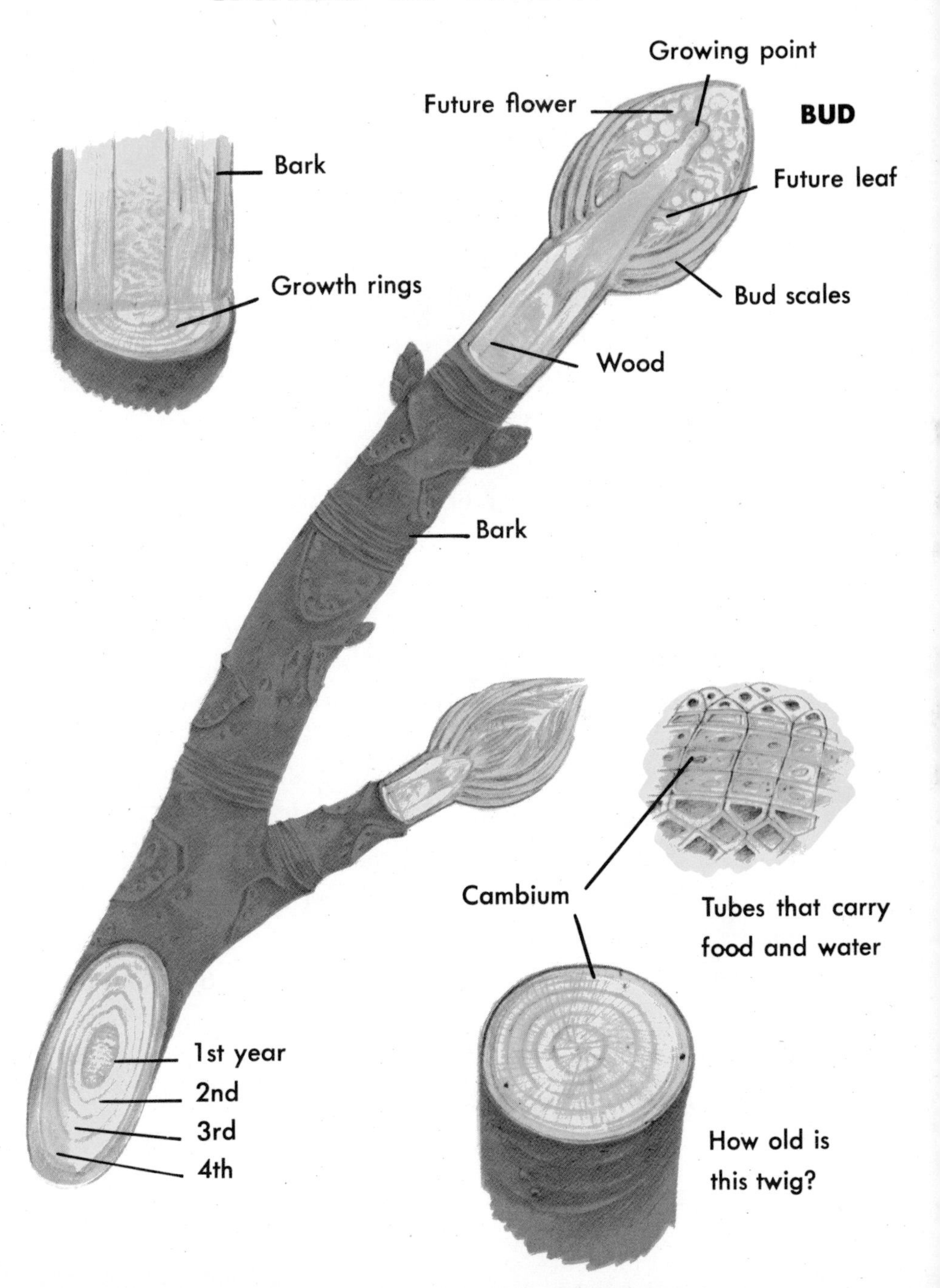

All lumber comes from stems of trees. We also use other stems and stalks. We eat asparagus and celery, which are stalks. Though it grows underground, the potato is not a root but a swollen stem, full of stored food. The eyes of potatoes are buds. Cut a large potato into several pieces, each with at least one eye. Half bury the pieces in sand or soil in a shallow dish. Water, and watch the eye buds open into new shoots.

From other valuable stalks we get fibers to make rope, and flax to weave into linen cloth. Some stems have, in their sap, chemicals we use. From the sap of the rubber tree we get latex to make rubber. Pine trees give turpentine and rosin. Sugar cane and sugar maples provide sugar. Other trees yield medicine, and the sap of the chicle tree of tropical America is made into chewing gum. Nowadays people are finding more and more uses for wood. Even sawdust is used, to make alcohol, and if it is properly treated, it can be made into food for cattle. Rayon cloth is made from wood. So are all newspapers.

The most important parts of stems are the tubes which carry water and food through the plant. If you cut across a corn stalk and look at it through a magnifying glass, you can see the ends of the tubes as clusters of dots. You can see the tubes at work if you get a fresh stalk of celery with leaves on top. Set the stalk in a glass of water colored with red ink. Look at the stalk the next day and the day after. See what happens. Cut across the stalk with a knife and see which parts are red.

WHAT'S INSIDE A ROOT?

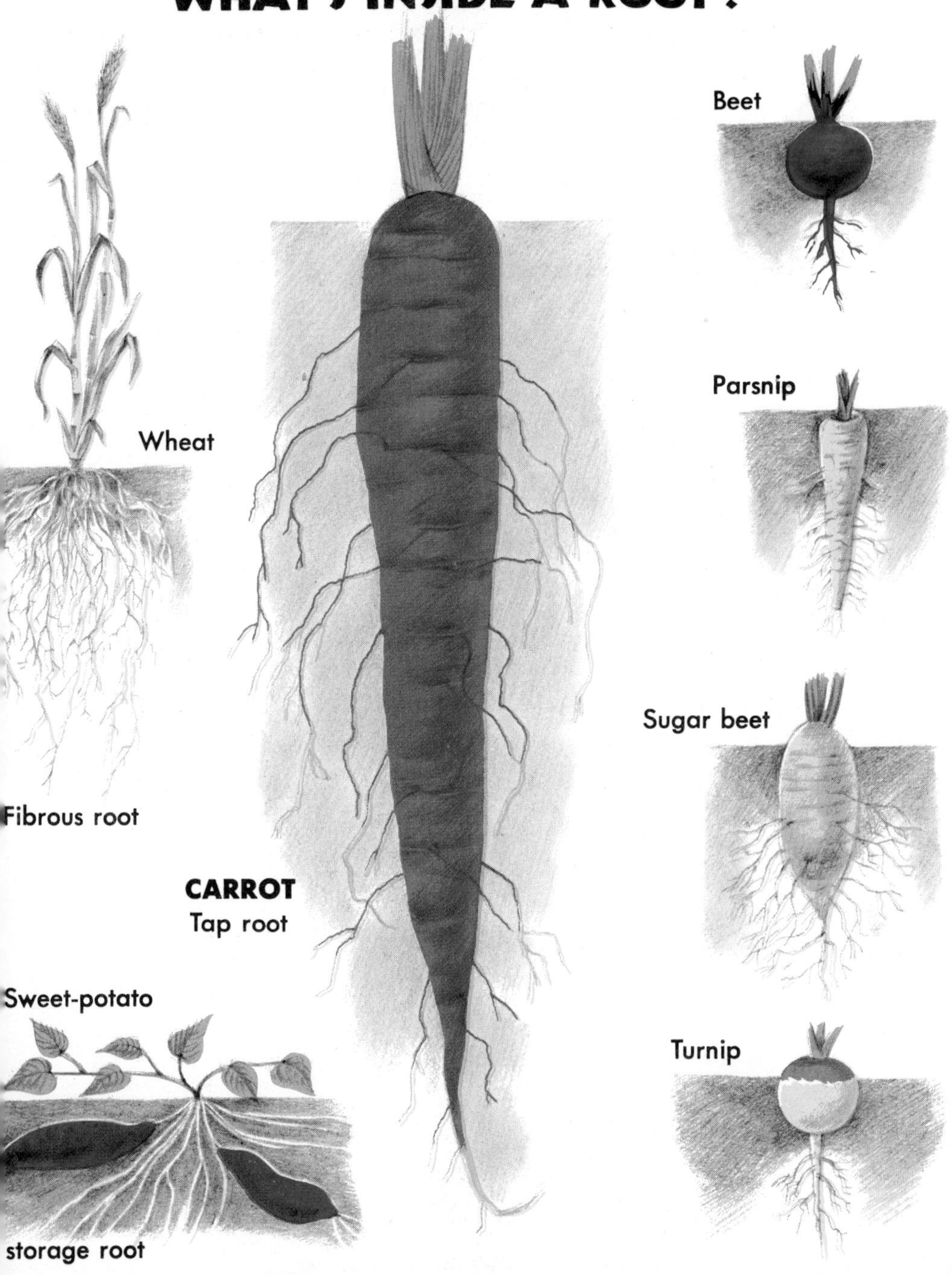

Plants need water to grow. The roots take it from the soil as the plant needs it. A few desert plants store water in their stems and roots. The roots you see when you pull up a weed are not all the plant's roots. Many more, smaller roots are left in the ground. With all its roots, a plant can get water even from soil that feels dry. Some plants store food in their roots and use it the next spring. These are the roots we use for food.

Desert plants that store water

INSIDE A CARROT

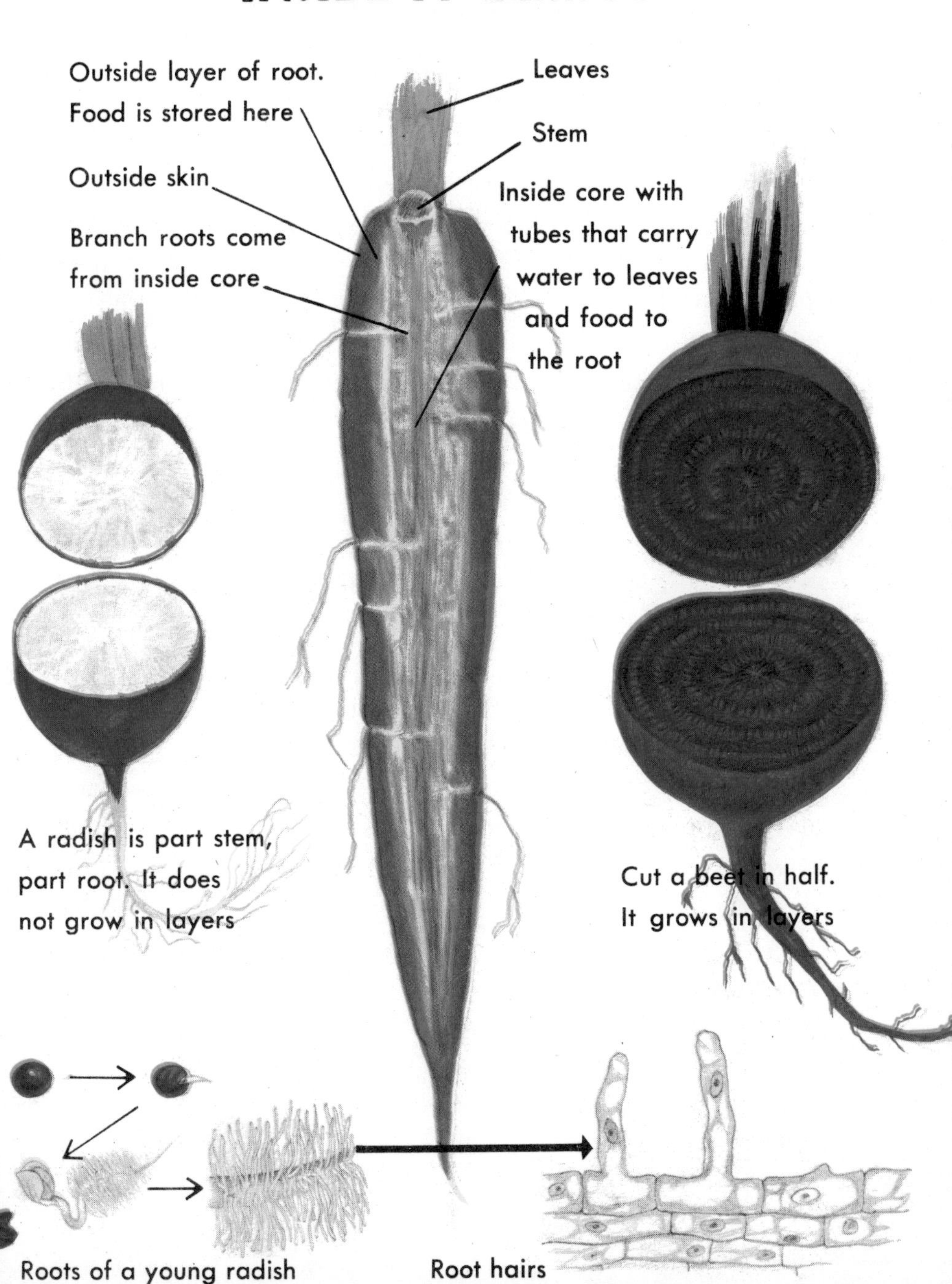

Plants have as many roots as branches, or more. The large roots divide into smaller and smaller roots till the smallest are fine as hairs. A man carefully measured all the roots of one rye grass plant which he grew in a box of soil about the size of an apple box. The largest roots of this grass, when he put them end to end, were over a block long. The next smaller roots came to over three miles in length. There were even more roots of the next smaller size, and these added up to over 100 miles. Finally he found over 200 miles of the smallest roots that could be counted. Altogether there were about fourteen million roots on this one plant.

Place a dozen or so radish seeds on a paper napkin or blotter in a saucer. Wet the paper and cover it with another saucer so your experiment will not dry out. Inspect the seeds day by day. See them split open and watch the roots grow. Use a magnifying glass. Soon you will see that the young roots are covered with a thick, white fuzz which is thickest near the tip of the root. The fuzz is made of many tiny root hairs, each growing from a single cell on the outside of the root. On a large plant the number of root hairs is beyond counting. Nearly all the water and minerals that go into a plant pass through the root hairs.

Stand a carrot with leaves on it in a glass of red-colored water. After a day or two cut the carrot open and trace the path the red water has taken. Follow the tubes, now colored red, from the branch roots to the main root, and up the main root to the stem and leaves.

WHAT'S INSIDE A FLOWER?

Not all flowers have bright colors. Those of most trees and grasses are small and green. Flowers make the seeds from which new plants grow. One part of the flower makes pollen grains. Another makes the tiny egg cells in the ovules that grow into seeds. These two parts are often in the same flower. They must join together before the seed will form. Many flowering plants die in the fall. Only their seeds remain alive to grow again next spring. These plants are called annuals.

INSIDE A FLOWER

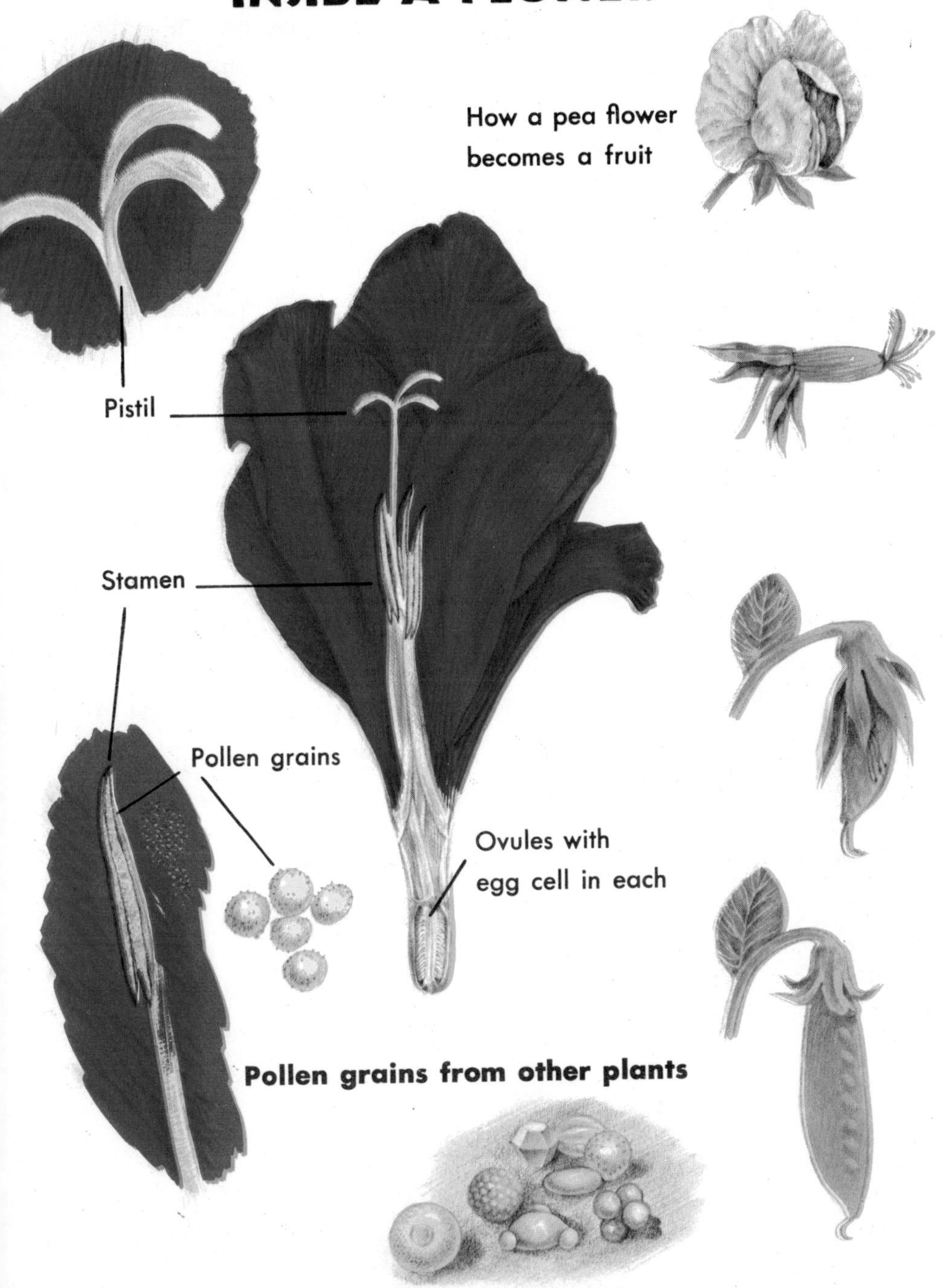

Flowers grow into fruits and seeds. There would be few new plants without seeds. Before a flower can make the seeds, pollen must reach the pistil of the flower. The pistil is the center part that has, deep inside of it, the egg cells of the flower. Some plants make a great deal of pollen. The wind carries the light pollen grains to other flowers. Plants that use the wind to carry their pollen, like oak trees, ragweed and many grasses, have small flowers without much color.

Insects carry the pollen of other plants from one flower to another. These plants have bright-colored petals, sweet odors, and even sweeter nectar to attract the insects.

Nectar is an insect food. Some bright flowers are shaped like tubes or tunnels. When an insect goes into the flower to get nectar, it has to brush against the pollen before it can get out. Then, when the insect goes to another flower, it carries the pollen along with it.

When pollen falls on the pistil or is carried to it by an insect, the pollen grain grows a tiny tube. This tube grows right down through the pistil till it touches an egg cell. Then a small living part of the pollen grain goes into the egg cell and joins with it. From then on, the ovule begins to grow into a seed. The egg cell divides into two cells, the two cells divide into four, and so on, till an embryo is formed. Meanwhile, the parts of the flower around the ovule change into the fruit.

Look at flowers to see the petals, pistil, and the stalks bearing pollen—the stamens. Use a magnifying glass so you won't miss anything.

WHAT'S INSIDE A FRUIT?

When the egg cells begin to grow, other parts of the flower near them begin to grow also. The ovules become seeds. The rest of the flower becomes the fruit. Sometimes there is a single seed in a fruit like a cherry or plum. Sometimes there are many seeds, as in grapes, apples, or oranges. Some vegetables are really fruits because they come from a ripened flower: beans, peas, peppers, tomatoes, squash. Nuts are fruits which are hard and dry. Many fruits are soft and juicy.

INSIDE COMMON FRUITS

Of all the parts of plants, we eat and enjoy fruits the most. Most of our foods from plants are fruits and seeds—not only the soft fruits like apples, pears, and grapes, but the grains, nuts, and melons as well. A watermelon or a pumpkin is just as much a fruit as an apricot, blueberry, or grain of wheat.

When the ovules begin to form seeds, other parts of the flower begin to form the fruit. Flowers with more than one ovule grow into fruits with more than one seed. Fruits form in different ways, depending on the kind of plant. In peas and beans, the fruit is a pod with the seeds hanging inside along one edge. In some plants the fruit is little more than a thin skin over the seed.

Besides the soft, fleshy fruits we eat in summer, there are other kinds that are hard and dry. The hard grains of corn, wheat, rice, and oats are one-seeded fruits which are dry when ripe. They are the most important foods in the world. Most nuts are fruits with a single seed, though peanuts often have two or three seeds.

Fruits and seeds are spread in different ways. When milkweed fruit splits open, the wind carries the small brown seeds away. Each seed has a tuft of silky hairs that serves as a parachute. Maple fruits have wings that spin them like a propeller, so they go farther before they fall. Cockleburs and other fruits stick to animals and spread their seeds that way. Some of the fruits you eat are not single but are really a cluster of many fruits growing close together. Pineapples, raspberries, and blackberries are this kind of fruit.

WHAT'S INSIDE A SEED?

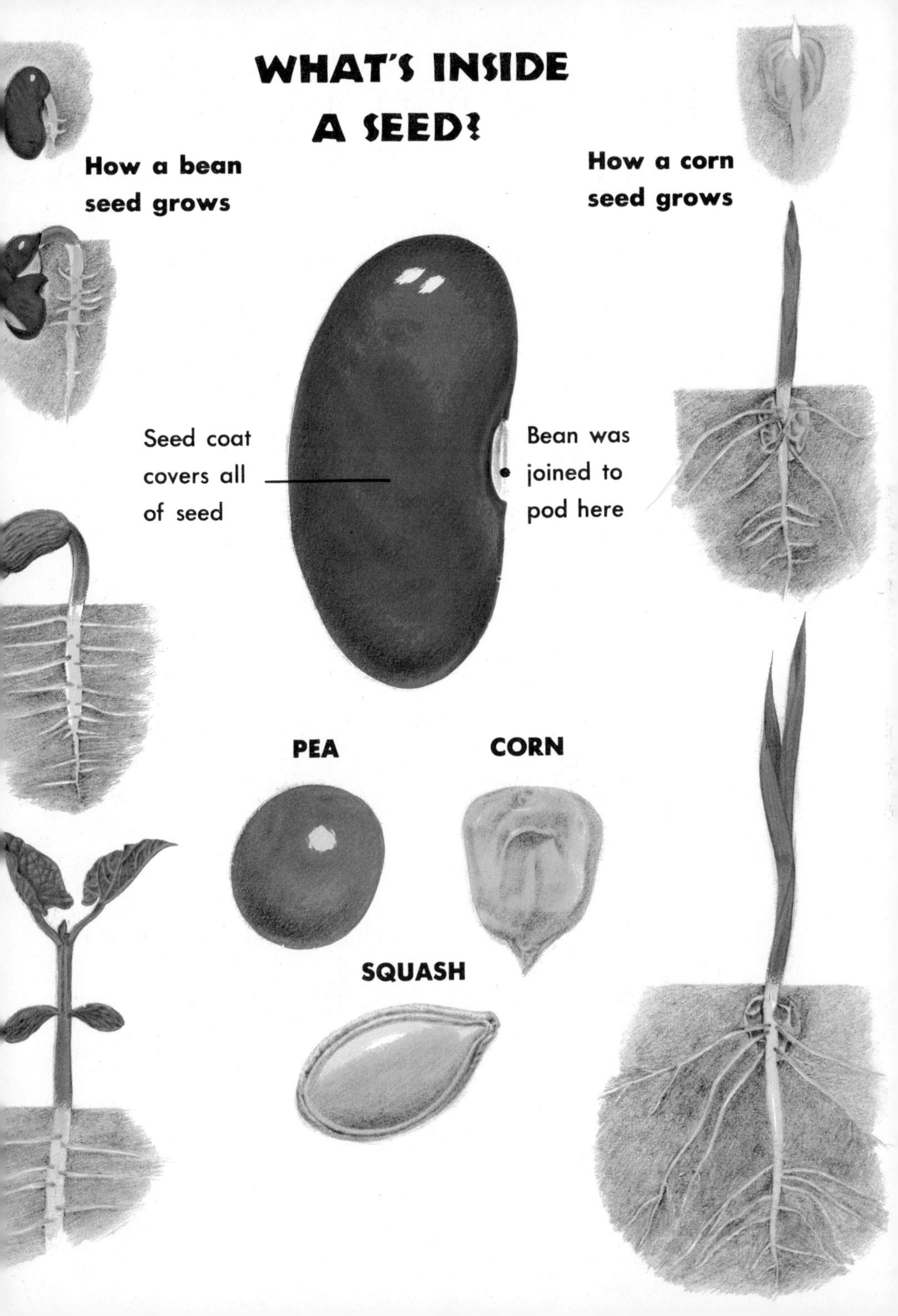

The new plant began when the egg cell inside the ovule started to grow. Inside the seed is a young plant, sometimes big enough so you can see its tiny leaves. As the seed ripens, the young plant stops growing, but it can stay alive in the seed for several years. When the seed is planted, the young plant begins to grow again. It puts forth a root, then a stem and leaves. At first it uses the food stored in the seed. Soon it can make its own food and store what it does not use.

INSIDE A BEAN

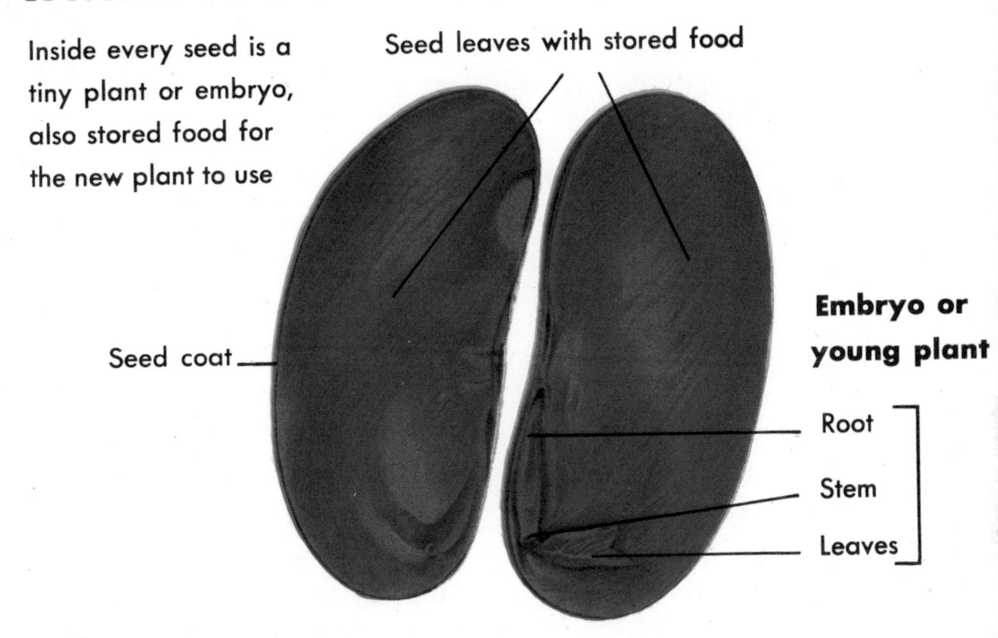

INSIDE OTHER SEEDS

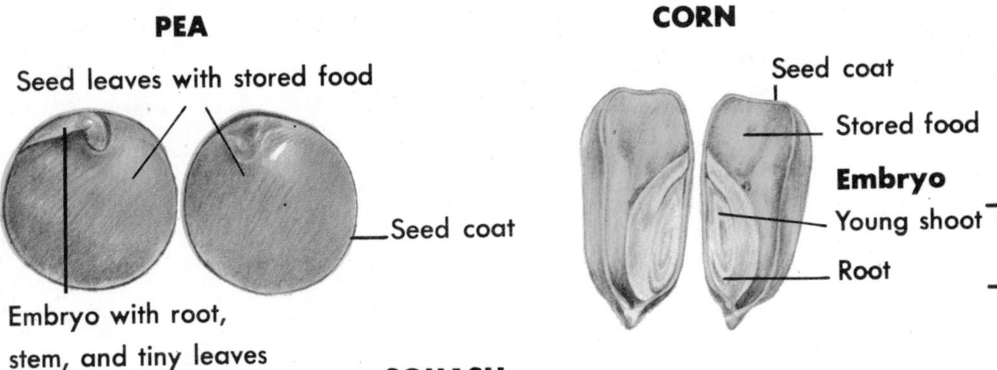

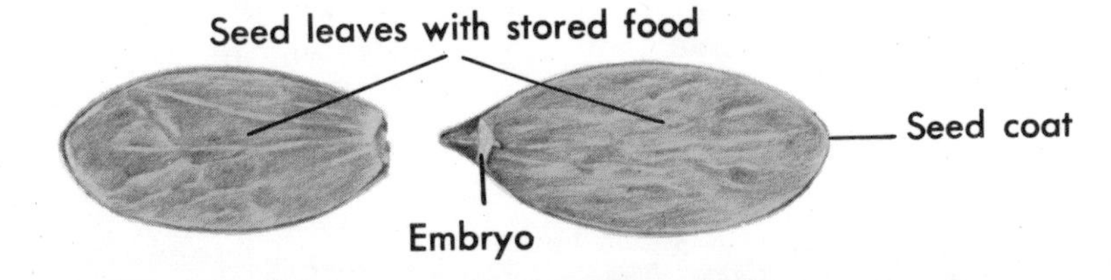

A seed is a storehouse of food. The young plant or embryo in the seed takes up very little room. The stored food makes up most of the seed. The resting embryo uses little food, but when the seed is planted and starts to grow, the food is used up rapidly. By the time the food in the seed is used up—in a week or two—the young plant already has roots, stem, and leaves and can make its own food.

Because seeds are so full of stored food, they are useful to us. Think of bread, cakes, cereals, and all the other good things made of wheat, corn, rice, or oats. Wild birds and small animals like seeds too. Weed seeds are an important food of birds in the winter.

Every now and then you will find seeds that have begun to grow while they are all still inside the fruit. Most of the time, though, seeds need a rest before they begin to grow. Some need both a rest and cold weather. These seeds will not grow till they have spent a full winter in the ground.

Place ten dry lima or kidney beans in a row. Measure how long the row is. Put these beans to soak in water and measure them again the next day. Overnight they have soaked up water and have begun to grow. Are they larger and is the row longer than yesterday? Curl a blotter or some paper towels around the inside of a drinking glass. Push some beans and kernels of corn between the paper and the glass till they are halfway down. Now add just enough water to wet the paper. Keep it wet. The seeds will grow and you can watch them.

OTHER WAYS PLANTS GROW

Most flowering plants grow from seeds, but some have found other ways of starting new plants. Sometimes a root may grow into a new plant; or a plant may grow from a stem or even a leaf. Some flowering plants, like bananas, do not make seeds that will grow. Bananas grow from shoots, or suckers. These are small plants that grow from the bottom of the stem of older plants. If you want to see a new plant growing from a root, do this. Put a sweet potato, which is a thick root, into a glass of water so that half is in water and half is out. Soon an attractive vine will begin to grow.

Stems may take root and form new plants. Cut a stalk of geranium about four inches long. Pinch off most of the leaves. Set the stalk in a small flowerpot filled with sand, or sand and soil mixed. Water it as needed and keep in a sunny place. The stalk will take root and you will soon have a new geranium.

Some plants make bulbs, which are short stems surrounded by a ball of thick leaves full of stored food. An onion is a bulb. Lilies, tulips, and hyacinths grow from bulbs too. When bulbs are planted, the stem at the center grows into a new shoot with leaves on top and roots below.

Plants, like all living things, are made of many very small cells. Each cell is alive and does its

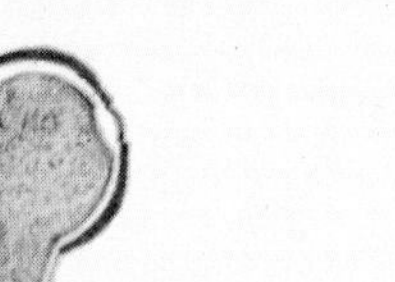

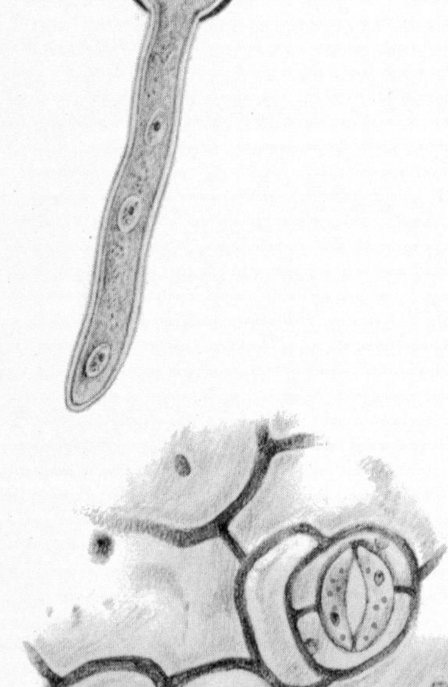

Pollen with tube

Food-making cells of leaf

Skin cells of leaf with guard cells

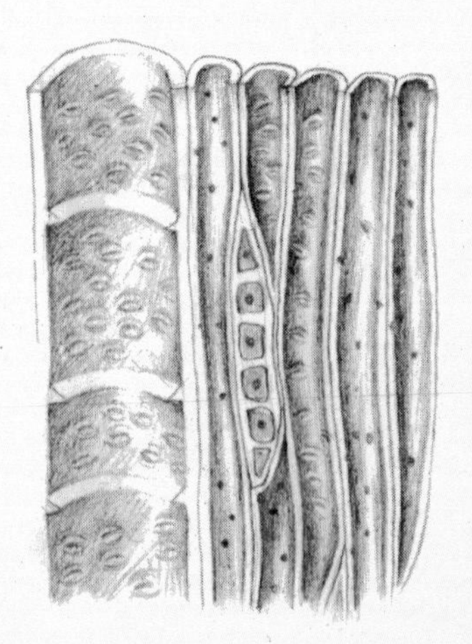

Wood cells

Grungy grime!
...and slime.
Climb!
Time!

What words rhyme with **sheep**?
Noisy cars that go "**beep**"!
A ballet dancer's **leap**,
And a trash heap to **sweep**.

What words rhyme with **go**?
I bet that you **know**!
There's a boat you can **row**,
And cars that go ***slooooow***.

FISHY WISHE
Uh, Oh!
Look, I'm on tippy-toe!

Let's make rhymes for **purple**!
Maybe birds that go **chirple**?
A big Barkley **slurple**,
Or baby's first **burple**!

What rhymes with **icky**?
Bubblegum that is **sticky**,
A game that is **tricky**,
And dogs who are **licky**.

Which words sound like **zap**?
Fairy wings going **flap**!
And the shoes that you **tap**
To the beat—as you **snap**!

Hi, everybody. We just poofed over from Sesame Street.
Oh, no– not a-g-a-i-n!
What rhymes with **tumble**?
Poor Jack's grumpy **grumble**,
Ginger cookies that **crumble**,
And bees that are **bumble**!

Do some words rhyme with **stick**?
Yes! A house made of **brick**.

A soft baby **chick**,
Or a camera to **click**!

What rhymes with **snowy**?
A new baby **joey**,
A pretzel that's **doughy**...
And don't forget **Zoe**!

All baby kangawoos are called joeys, like baby bears are called cubs.

What rhymes with **tub**?
Well, there's **scrub-a-dub-dub**,
And a miniature **sub**,
Or one baby bear **cub**!

PARTY ¡FIESTA!
What rhymes with **fiesta**?
I know *la respuesta*! A basket—*la cesta*. And *una siesta*.

Rosita told me *la respuesta* means "the answer" in Spanish. And *la siesta* means...
Elmo knows that! It's a lunchtime nap!
It's noon. Ernie'd better get here soon.

Elmo will tell Dorothy you said hello!
I didn't know fish could glow. That is sooo magical!
Did You Know

What rhymes with **nose**?
Snuffleupagus **toes**,
A swishy fish that **glows**!
And the bubbles it **blows**.

What words rhyme with **sloppy**,
Like Oscar's **Jalopy**?

Bunnies all **hoppy**
With ears that are **floppy**.

Okay, Slime-o, I'll read a bedtime story. But it's gotta be grouchy!
Let's find rhymes for **story**!
Like a lion who's **roar-y**,
A monster who's **snore-y**...
And space that's **explore-y**!
TRASH GORDON
SPACE GLORY

And what rhymes with **bug**?
Why, a nice slimy **slug**,
Who's all tucked-in and **snug**—
Or the tiniest **hug**.
An itsy-bitsy pajama party!
Is that not adorable?

And last, what rhymes with **tabby**?
A blankie that's **shabby**,
A fairy named **Abby**,
And the family **Cadabby**!

What Makes You Giggle?

By P.J. Shaw
Illustrated by Tom Brannon

What makes you giggle,
What gives you a grin?

Big Bird in a tutu doing a spin!

What makes you chuckle,
Or tickles your tummy?

A grouch birthday party—
Where presents are crummy!

Do giraffes give you laughs
On a trip to the zoo?
Or how about chimps?
Monkey-see, monkey-do!

A Snuffleupagus race
Might just give you a smile.

They *galumph* to the finish.
Alice wins by a mile!

What makes you laugh,
What makes you giggle?

A monstrous contest
For noses that wiggle!

Halloween's fun…
And so spooky, you shriek!
GO
AWAY

Hide-and-seek, trick-or-treat,
Oscar's can—EEK!
SCRAM!

What makes you whoop,
Makes you squeal with delight?
A day at the pool,
When the water's just right.

Dive rings and water wings,
Snorkels and masks.
Flippers and floaties,
And fountains that splash!

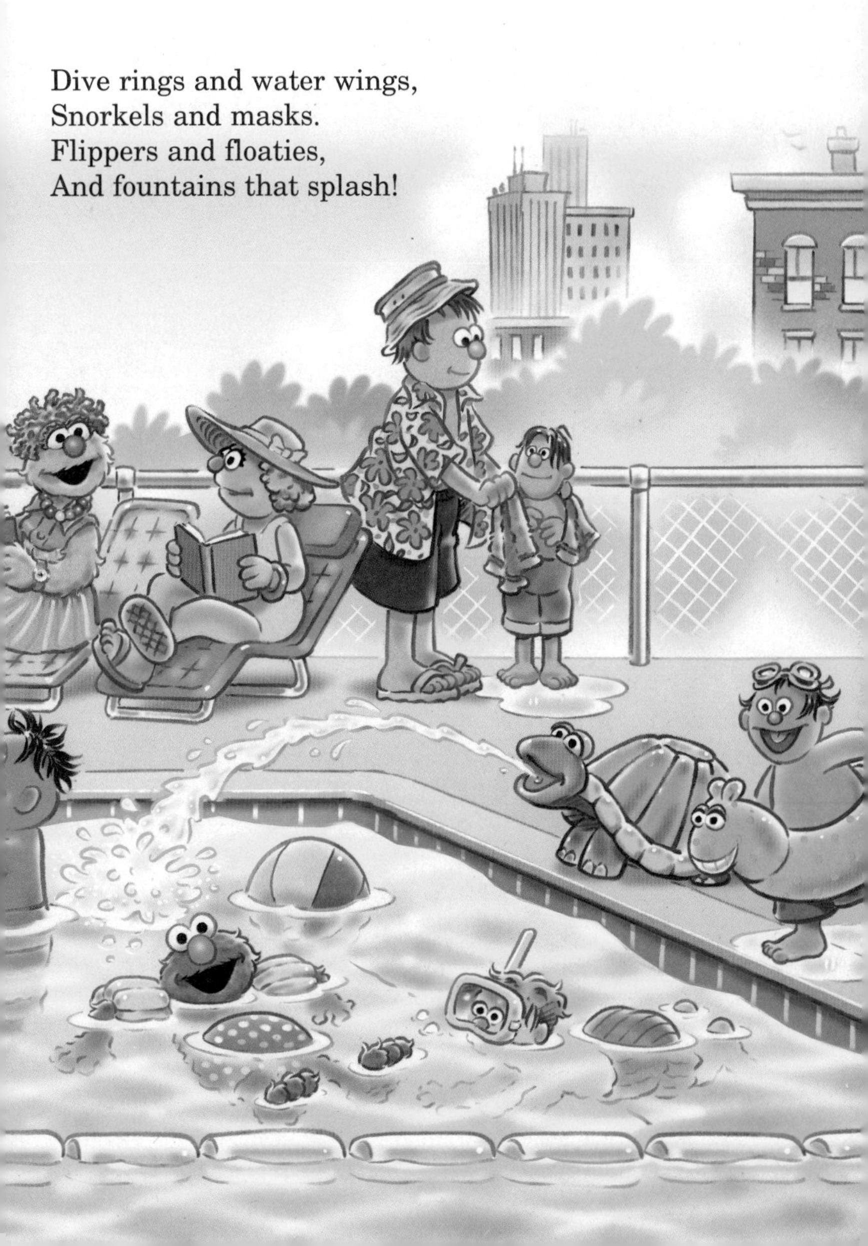

What makes you snicker,
Guffaw or tee-hee?
A neighborhood cookout
At Nani Bird's tree?

Make-your-own cupcakes
With milk-chocolate chips?
Maybe strawberries, raisins,
Or cinnamon bits....

Coconut, sprinkles,
Or butterscotch drops,
And pink-and-white frosting
To plop right on top.

What makes you goofy?
What makes you titter?
To trade silly faces
With Curly Bear's sitter!

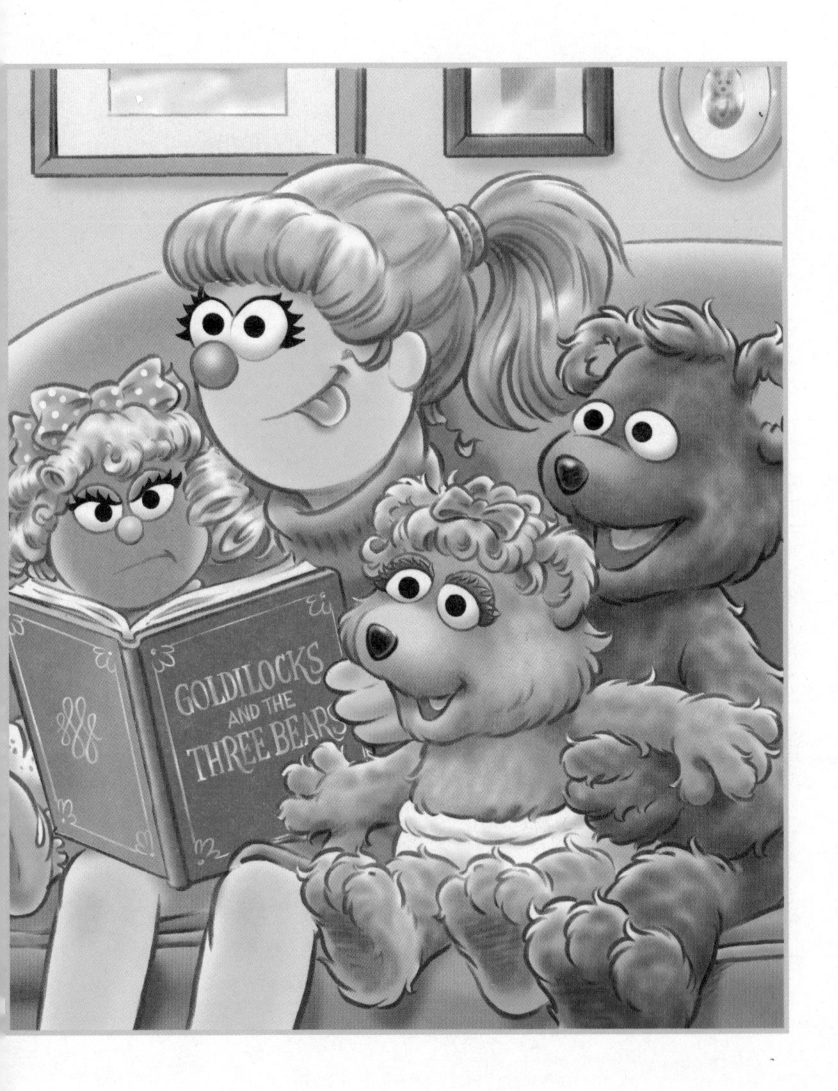
GOLDILOCKS
AND THE
THREE BEARS

A Twiddlebugs' picnic
With muffins and honey?

Or...an all-Grover rodeo—
Now, *that* would be funny!

What makes you giggle—
Makes you feel really good?
Just a regular day,
In your own neighborhood!